If a lion could speak, we would not understand him.

Ludwig Wittgenstein (1889–1951)

britta jaschinski

wild things

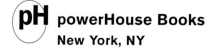
powerHouse Books
New York, NY

dear animals

once upon a time

nearly four billion years ago

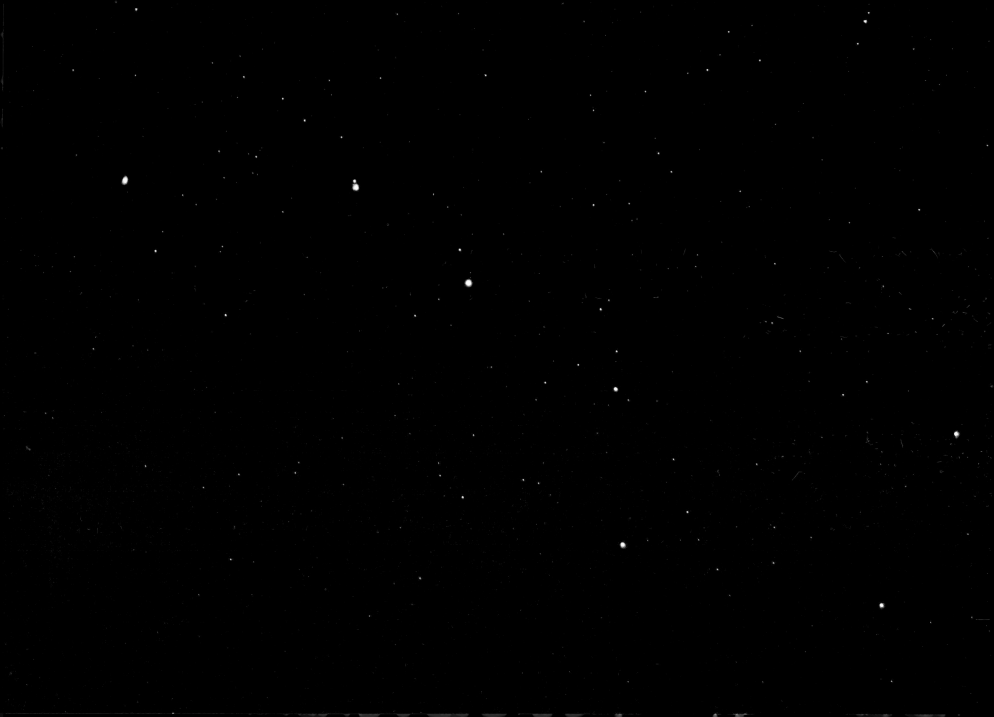

earth

was devoid of

life

when life did appear

t was first in water

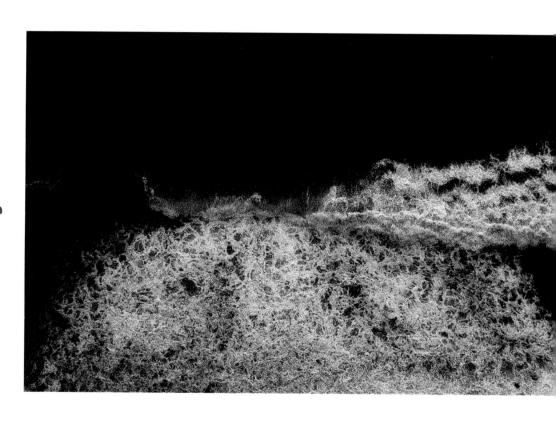

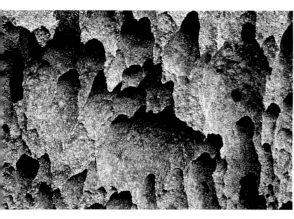 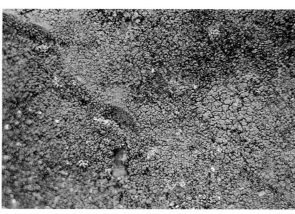 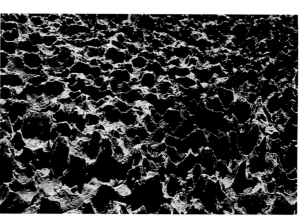 then..

higher organisms appeared which gave rise to more complex life

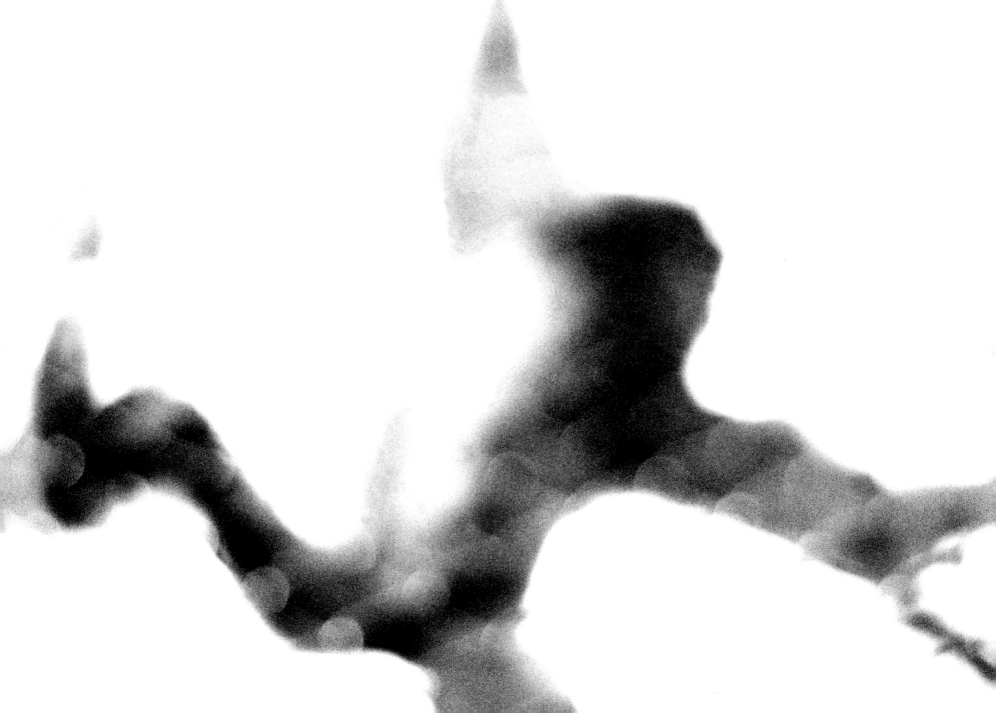

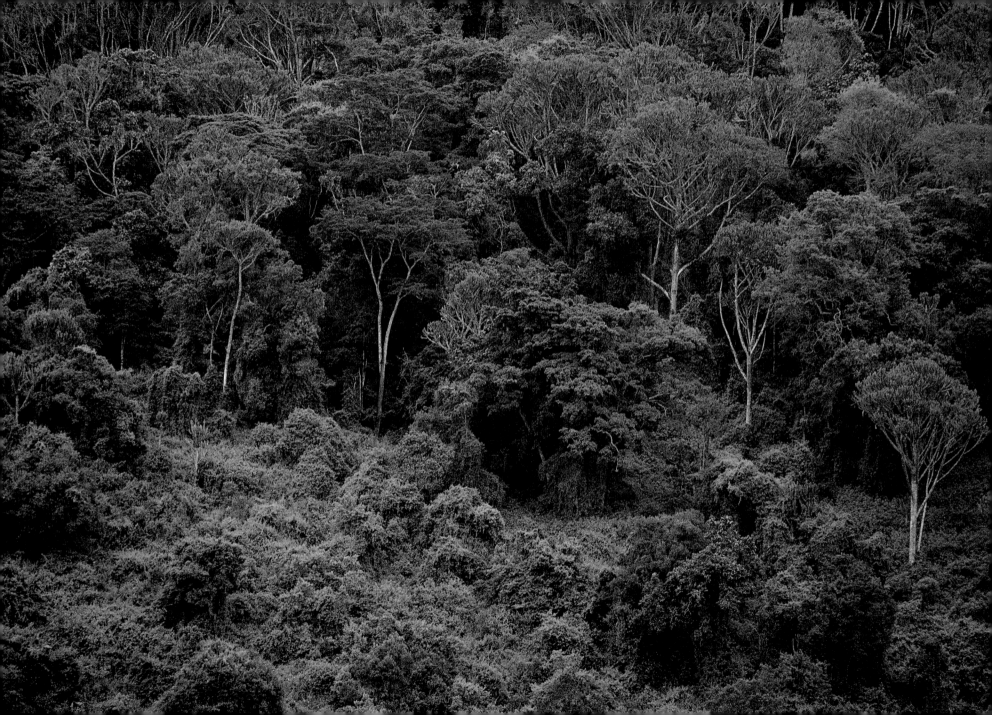

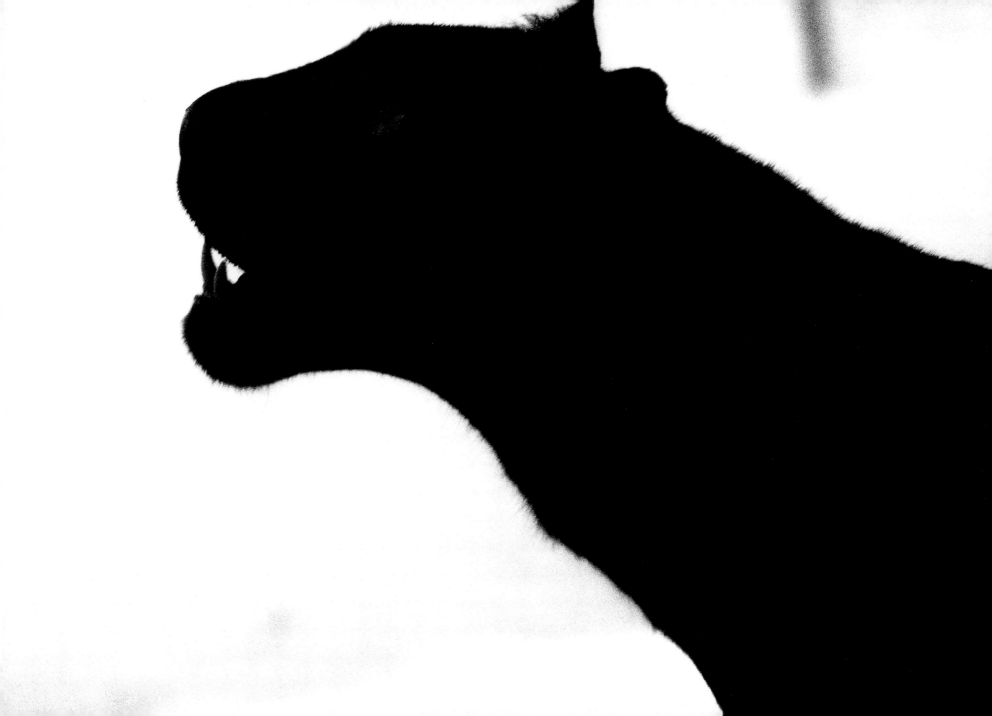

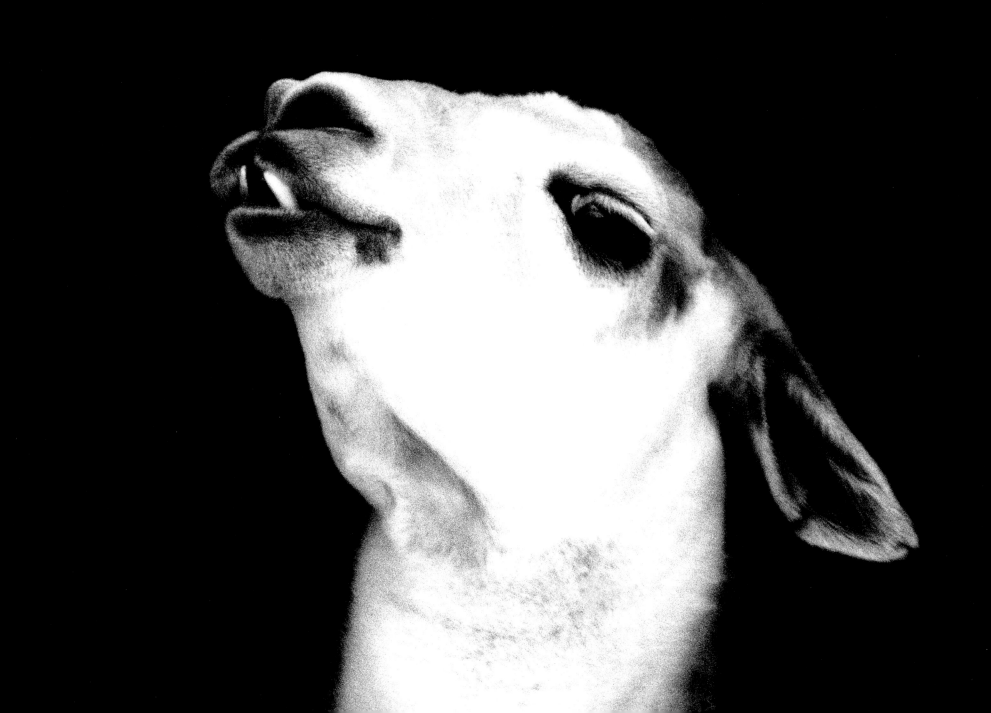

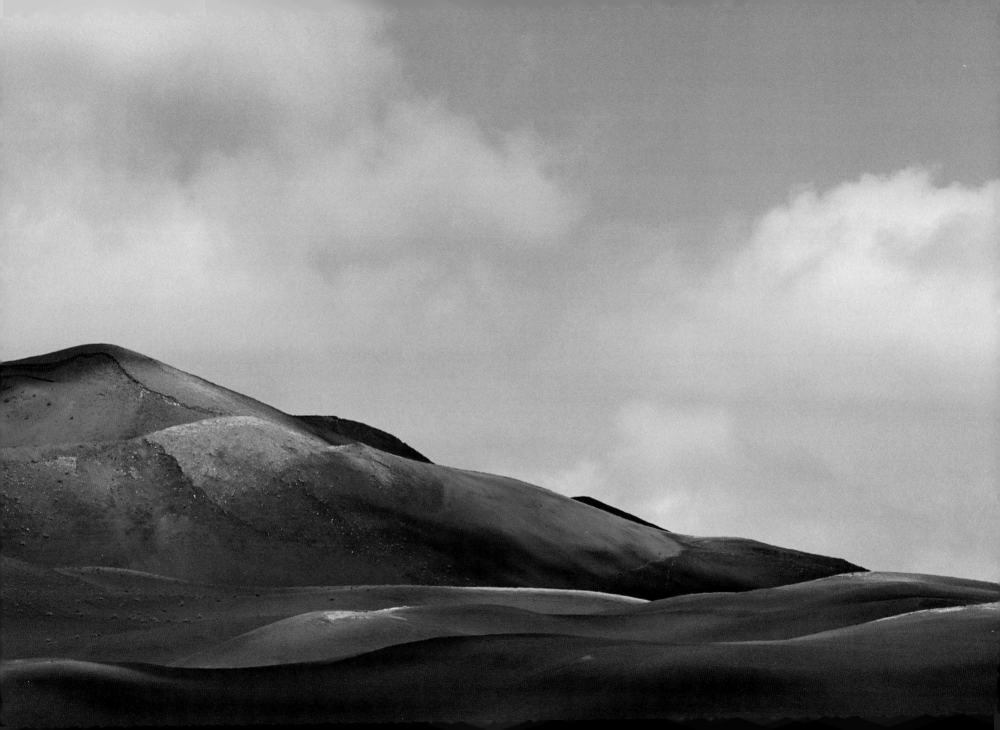

human existence

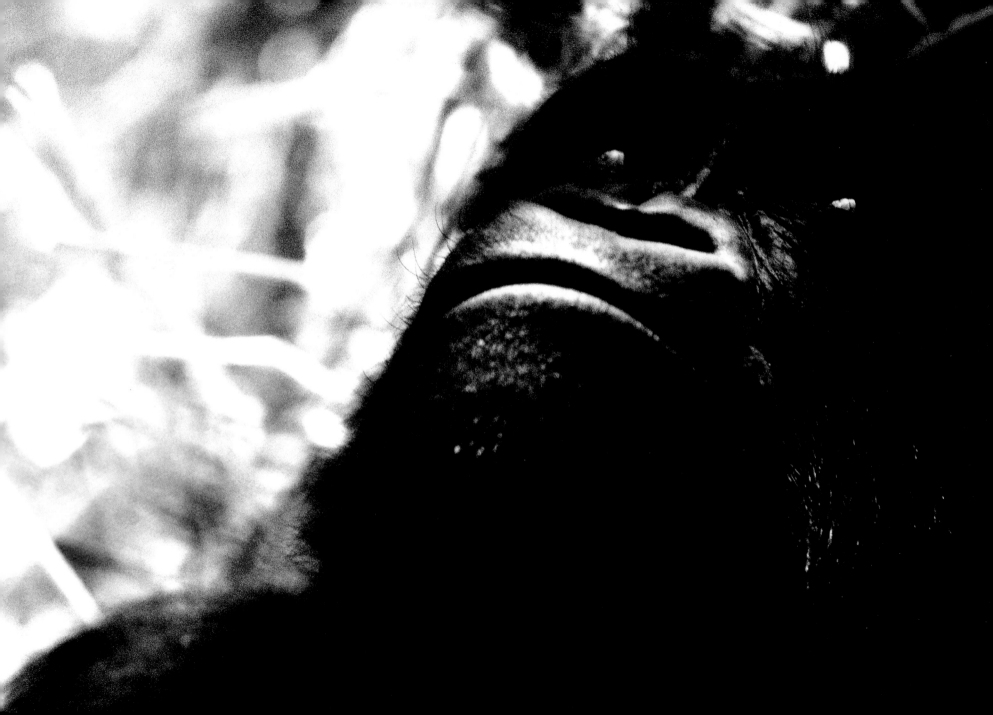

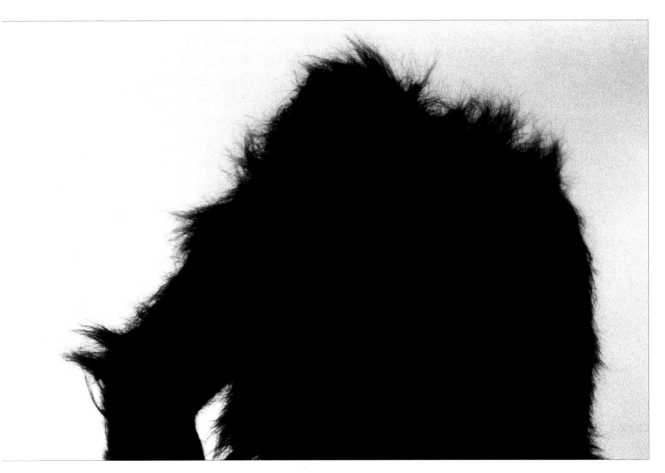

is purely accidental.

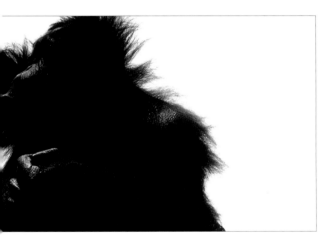
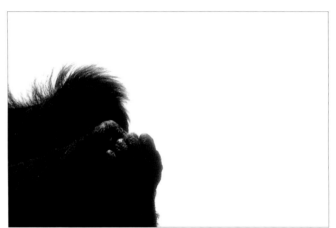
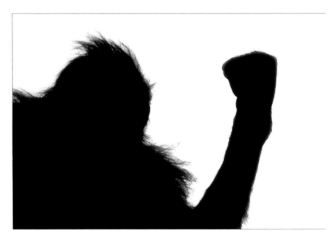

in the main we are part of what we call

nature

human numbers put great pressure and

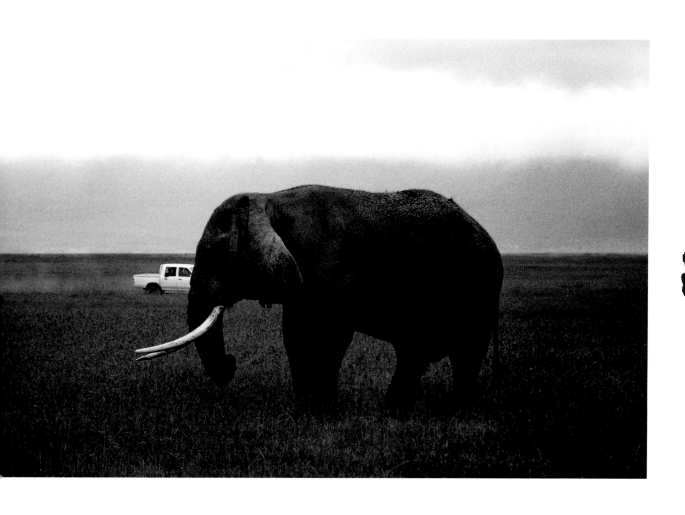

stress

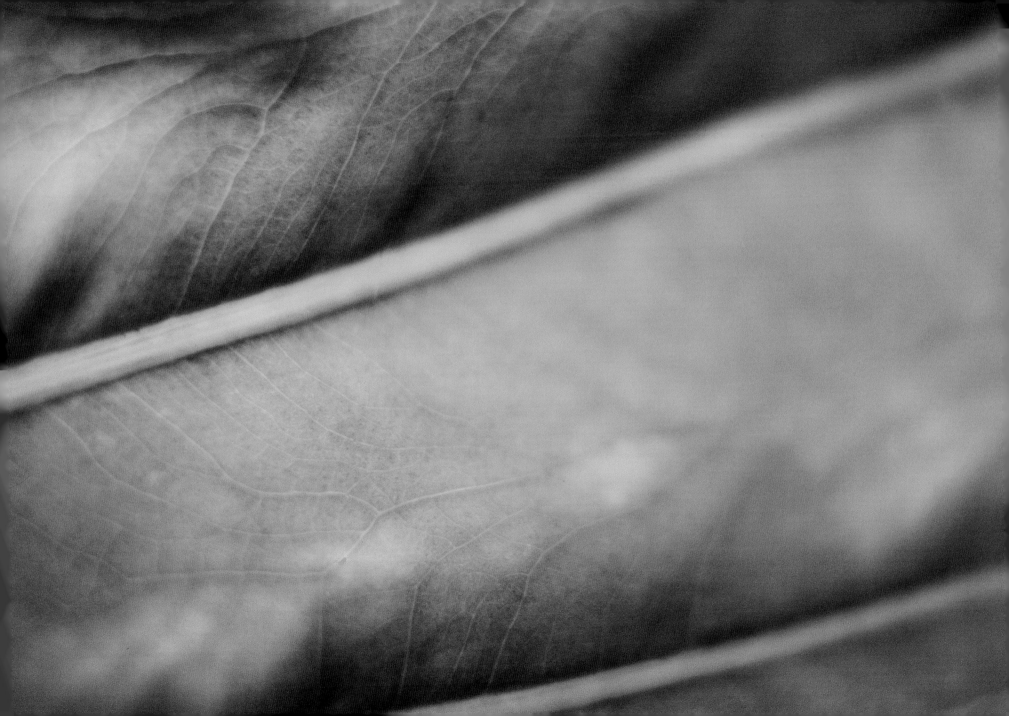

n the natural environment

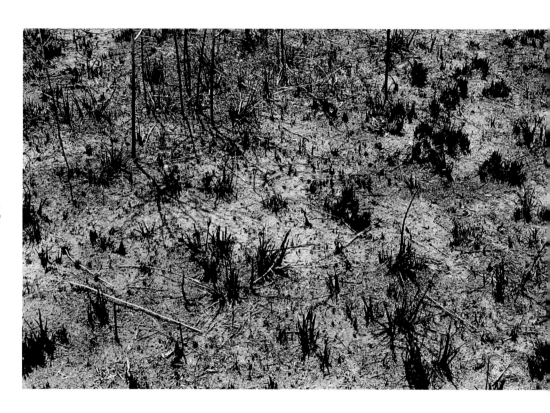

we should not ignore another extremely powerful

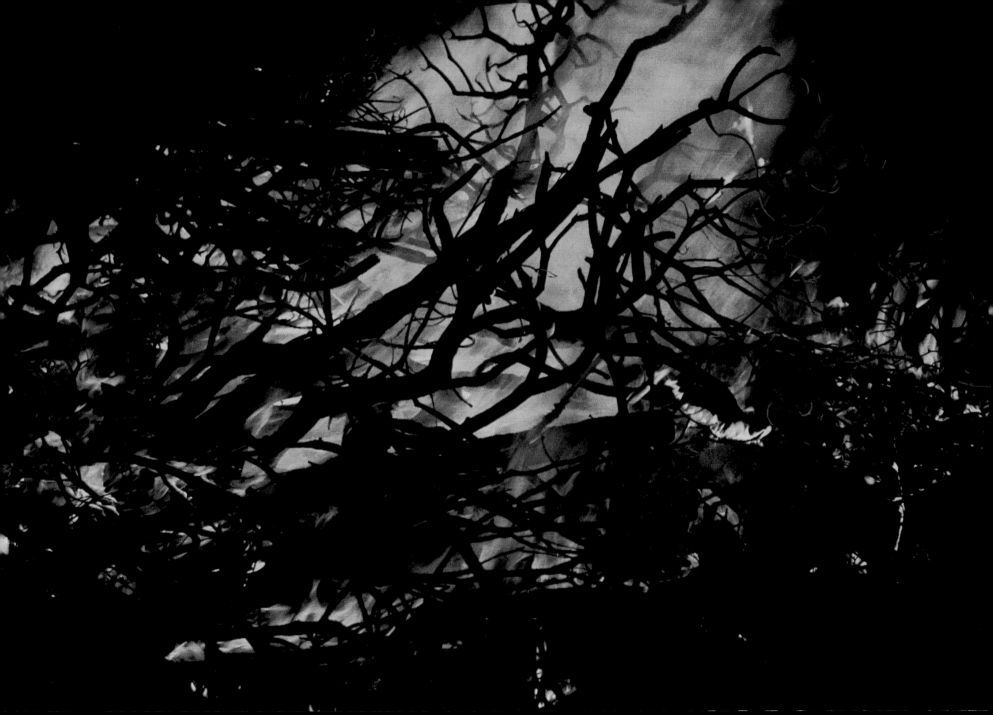

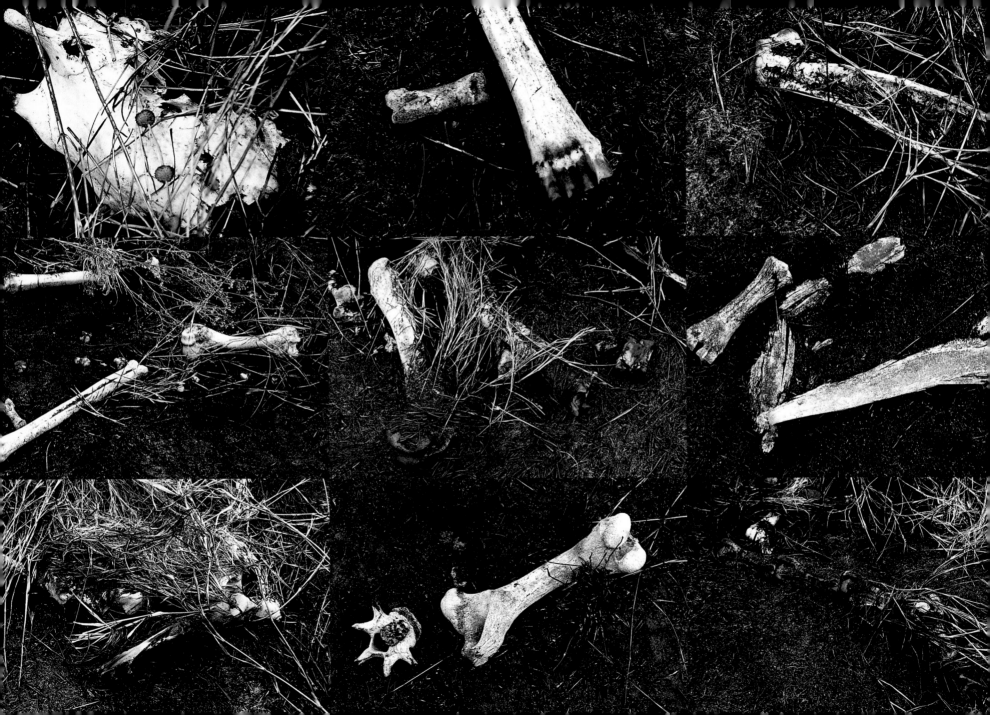

motivation

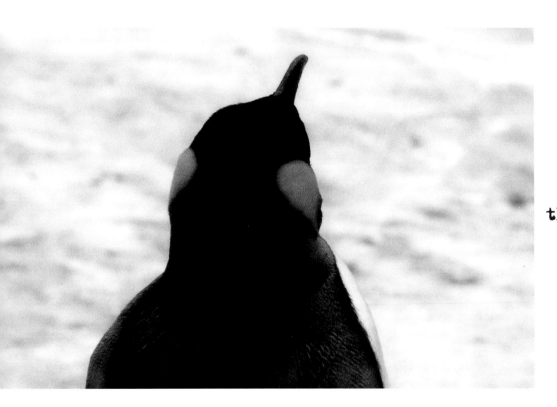

the aspiration to increase human welfare ar

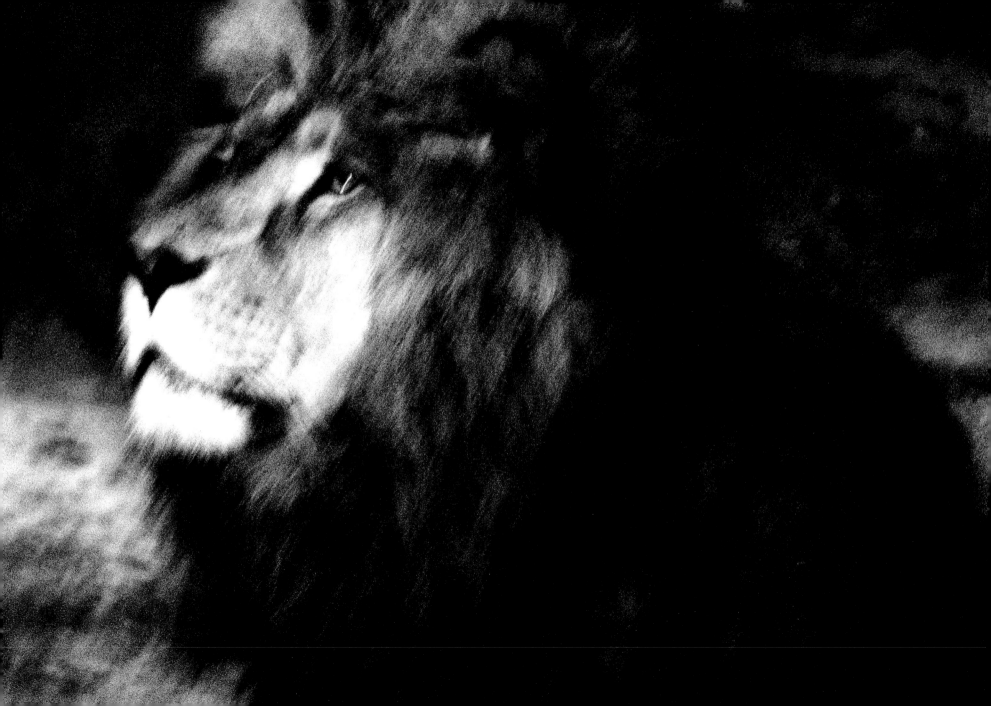

comfort

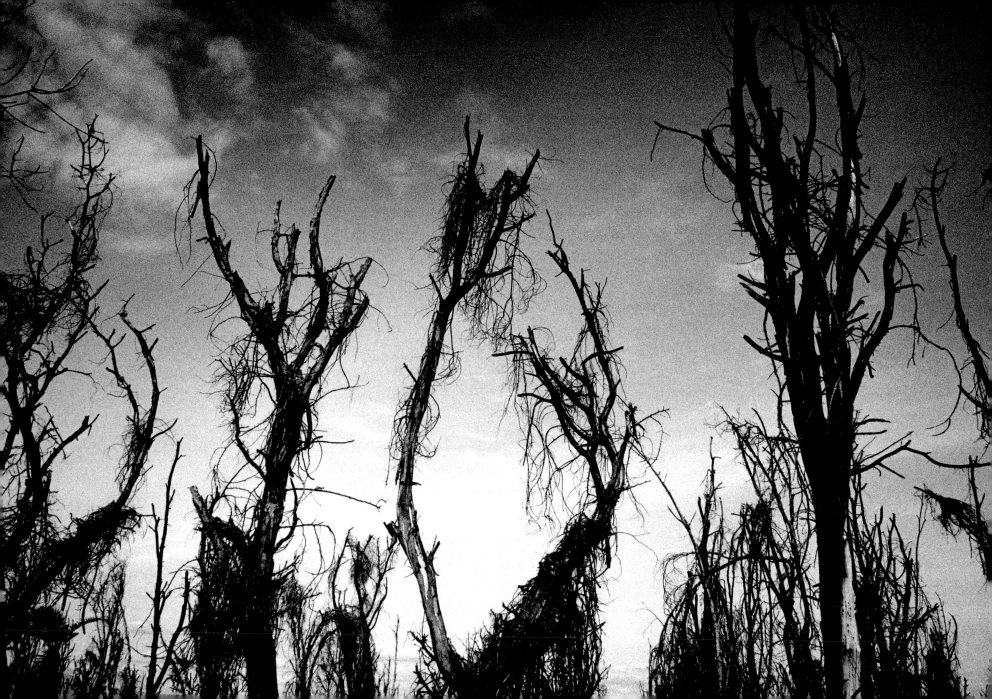

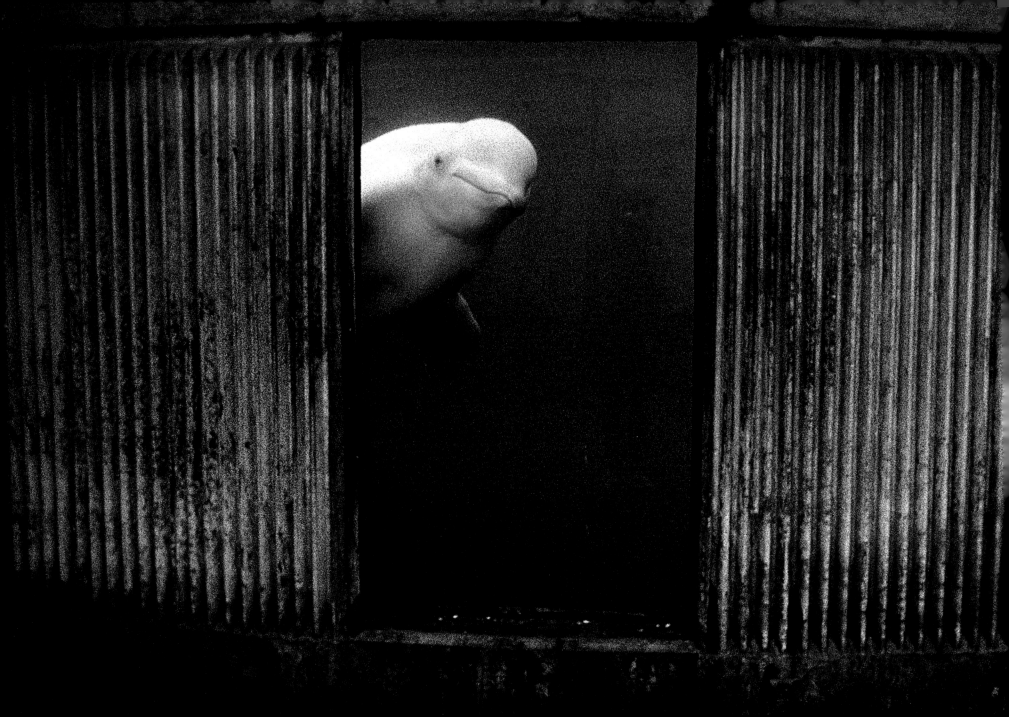

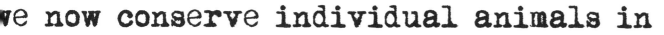we now conserve individual animals in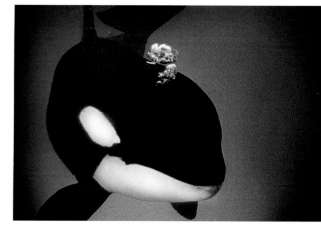

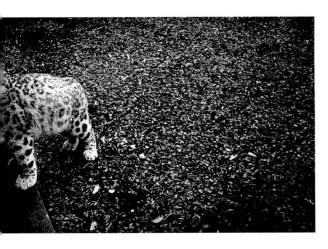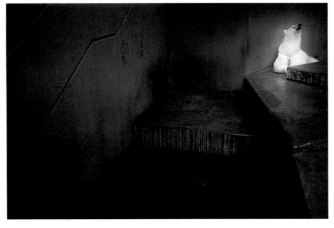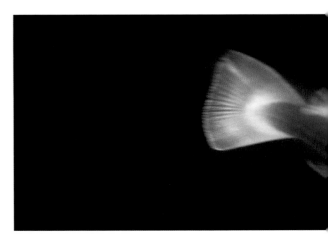

captivity

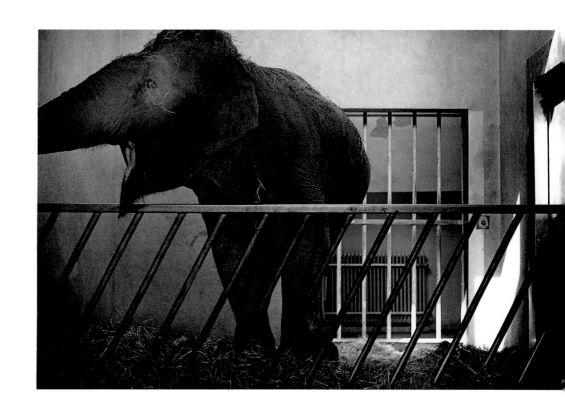

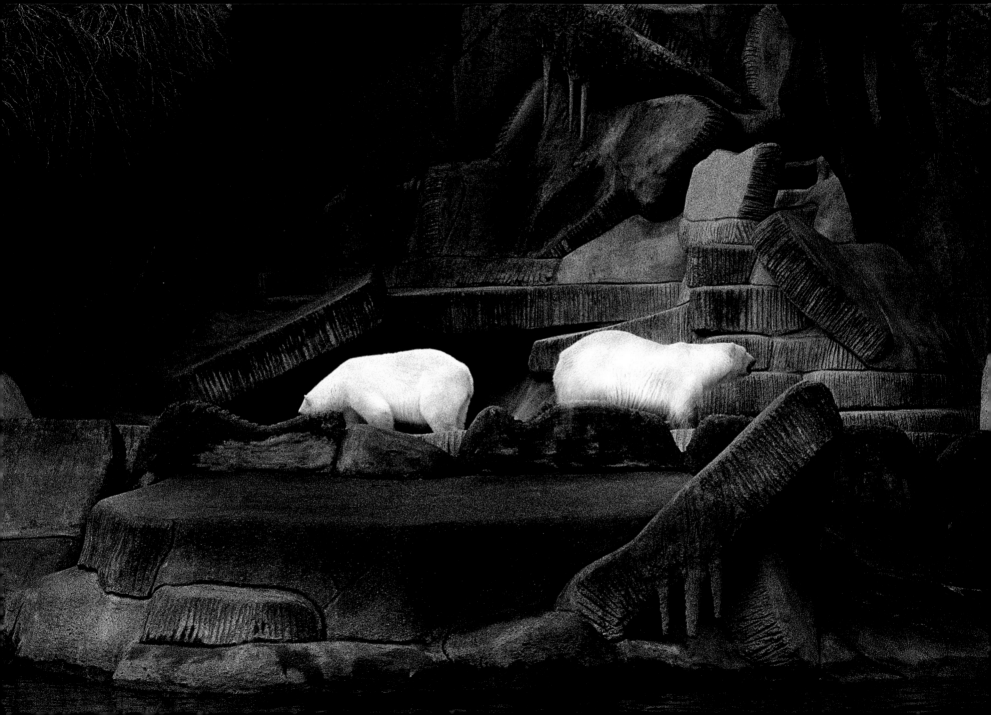

ut we do not protect your

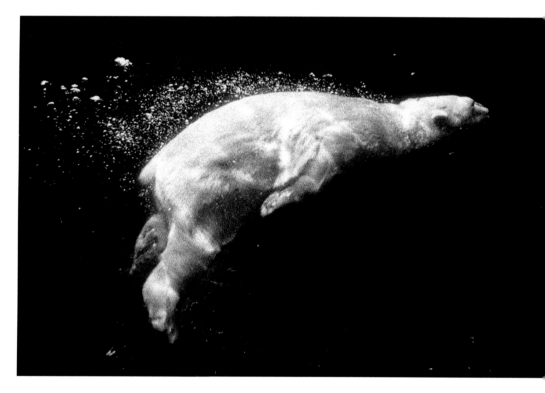

habitats

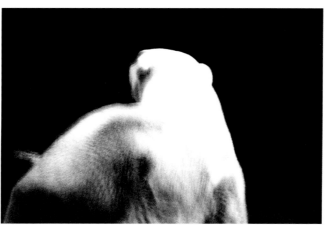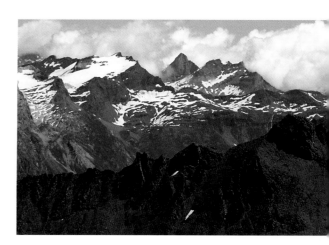

or the ecosystem

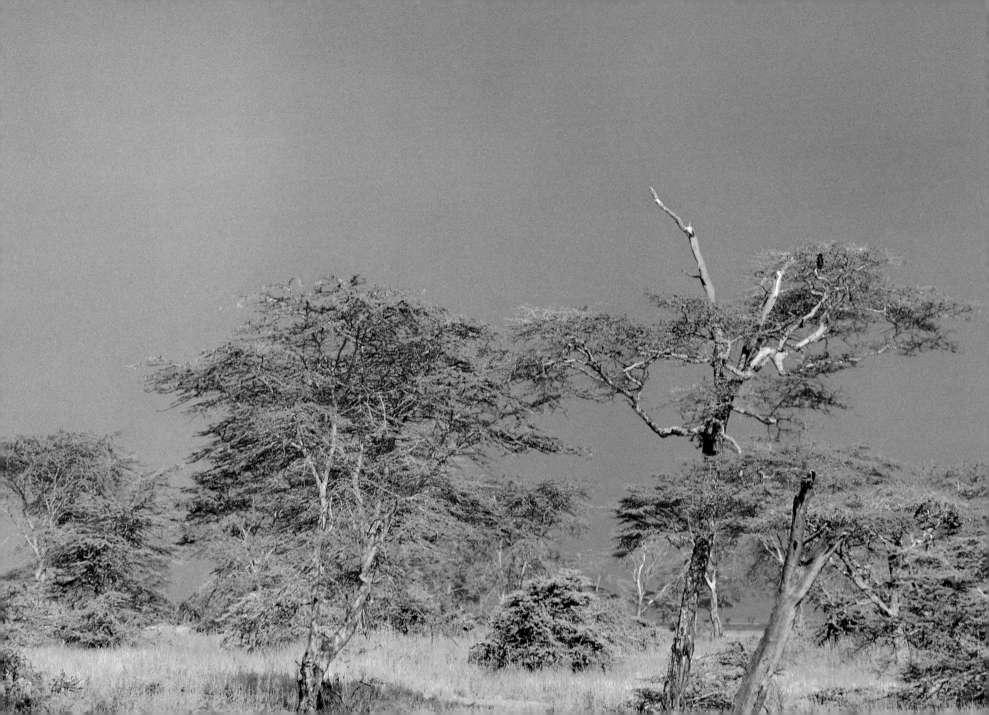

where will you

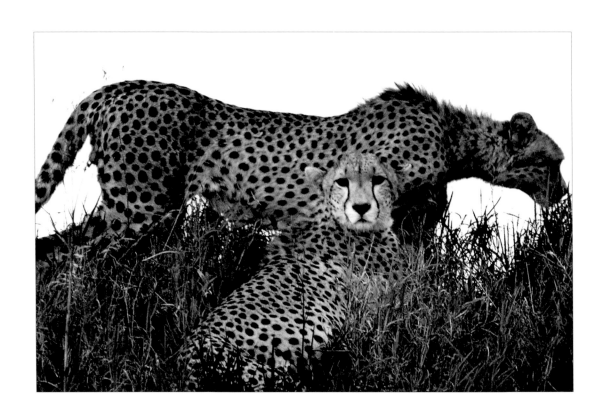

live

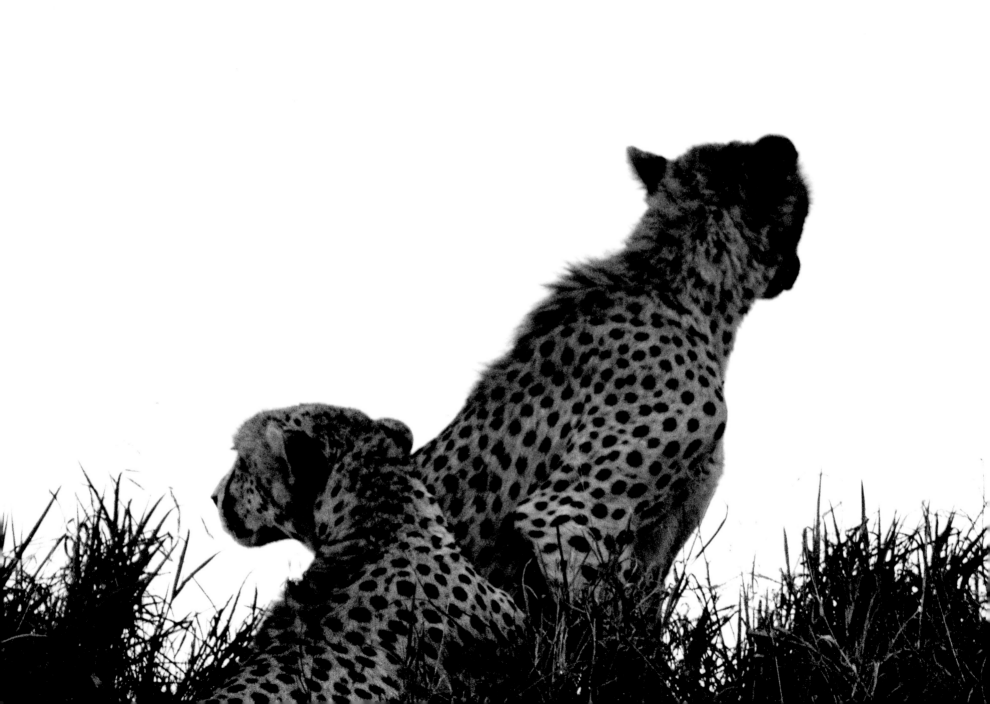

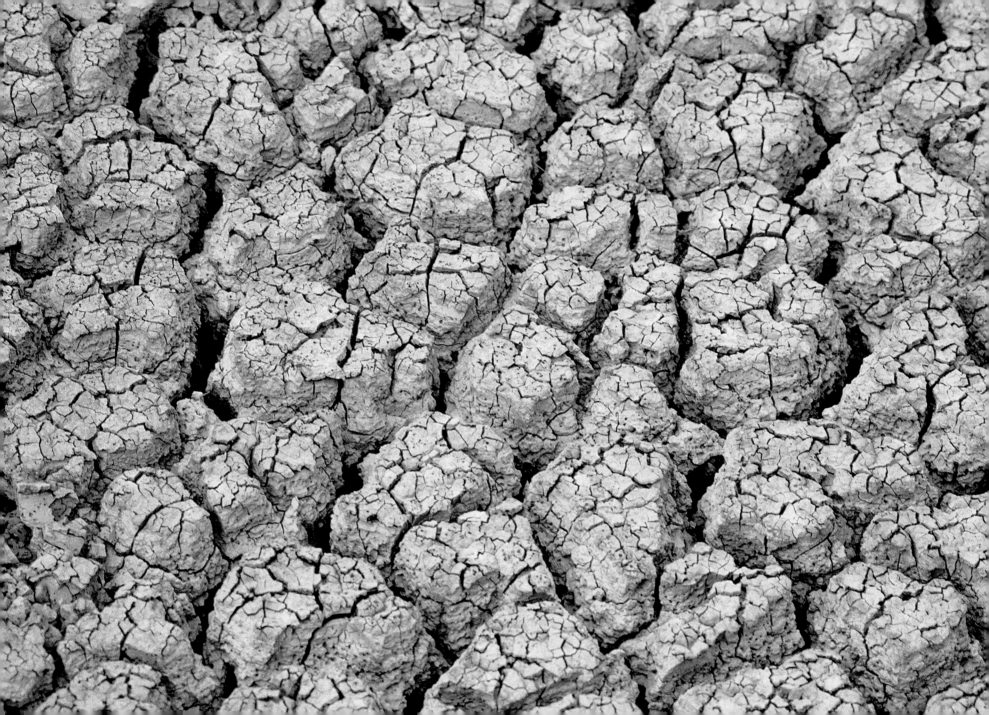

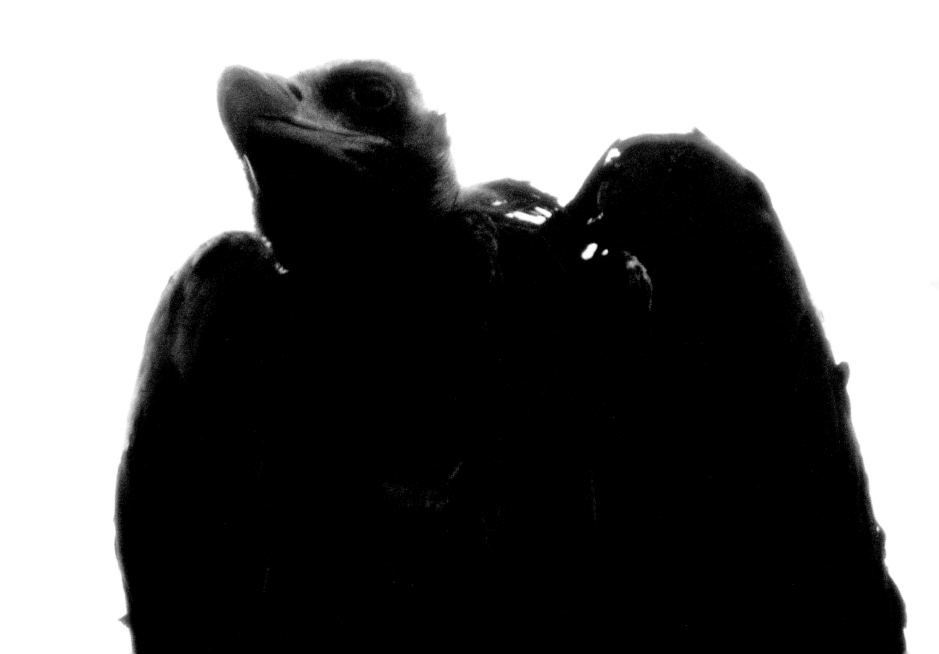

when we reintroduce you to the

wild?

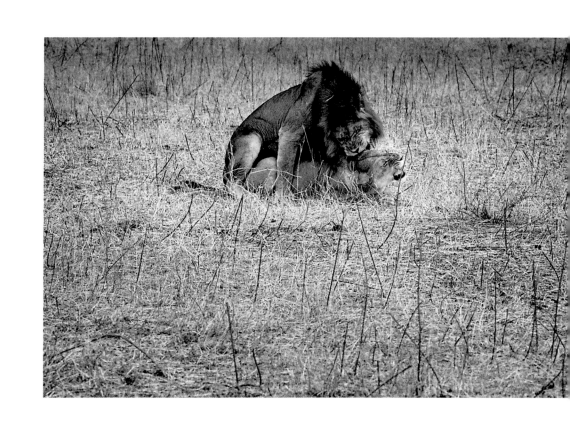

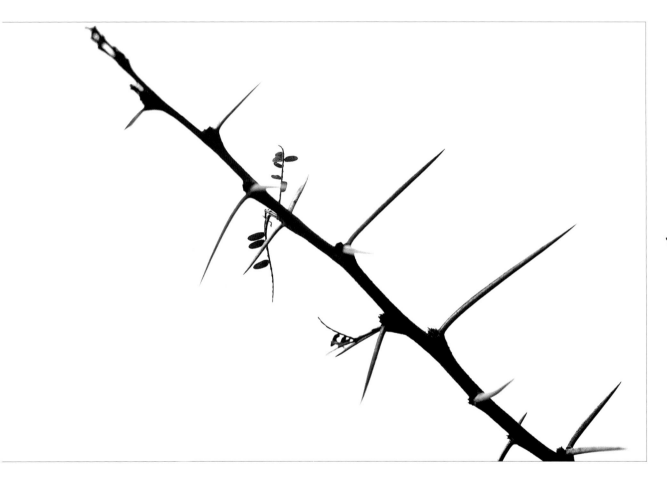

what will you eat

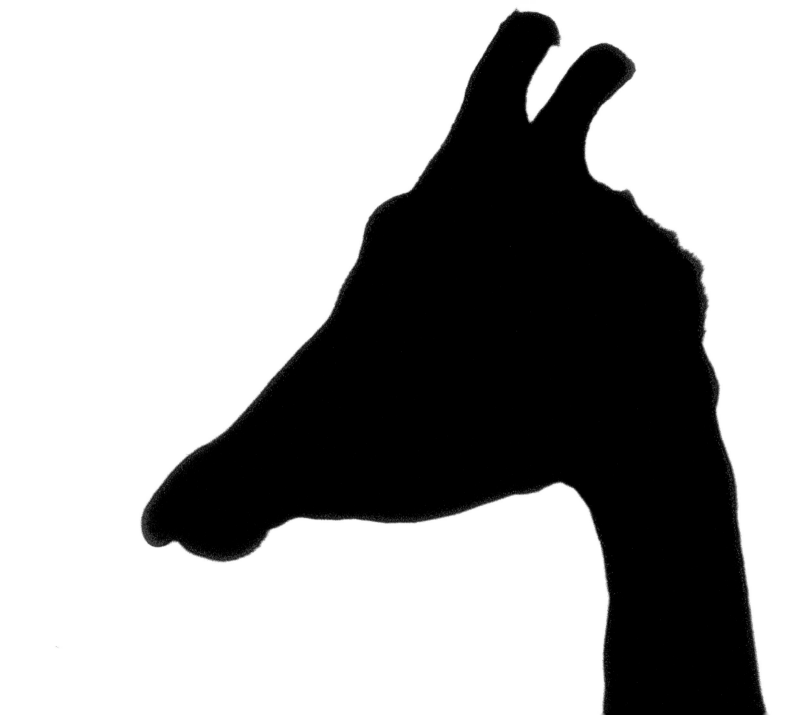

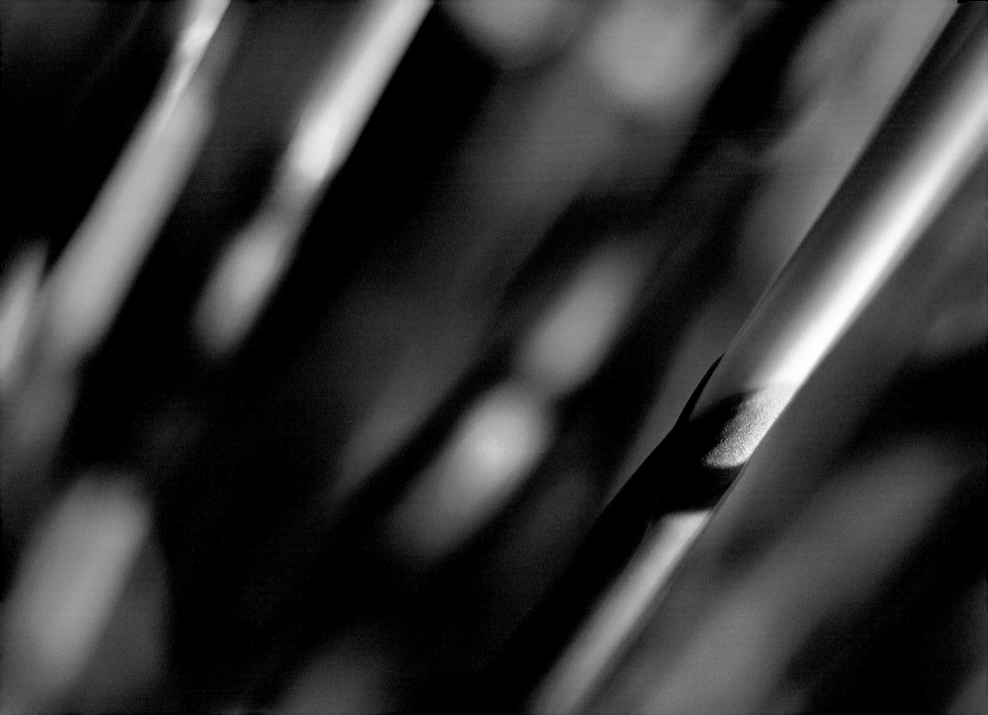

f the food chain has been systematically

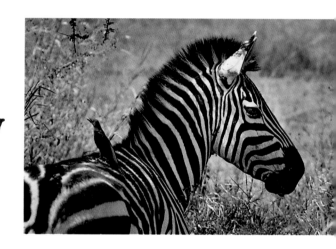

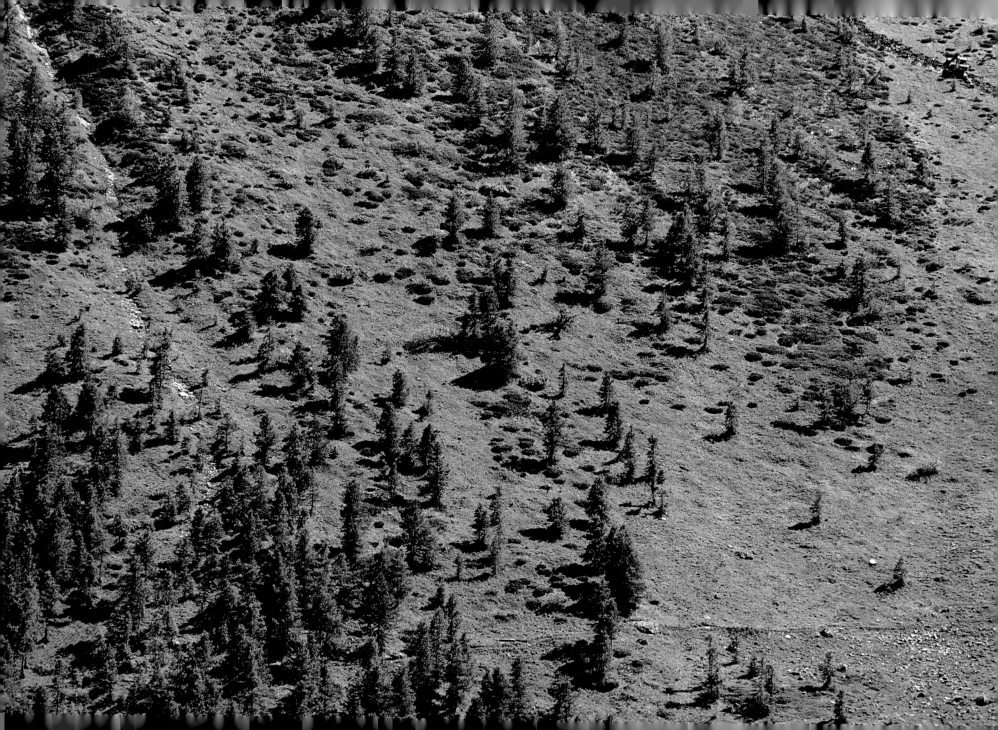

eroded?

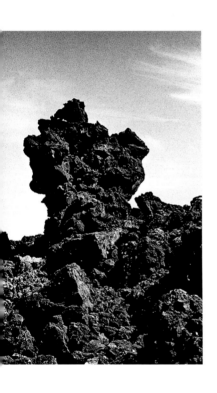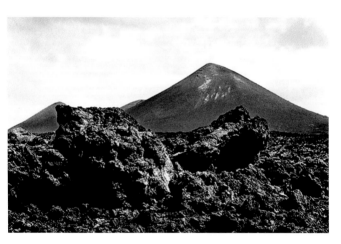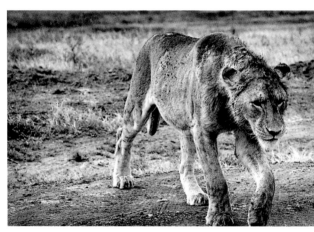

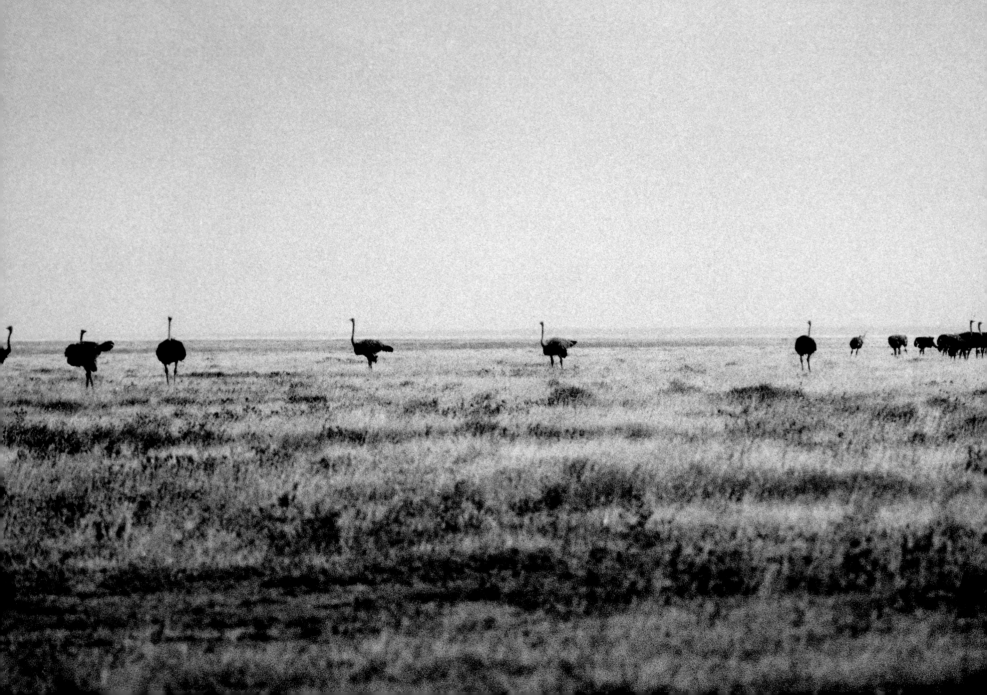

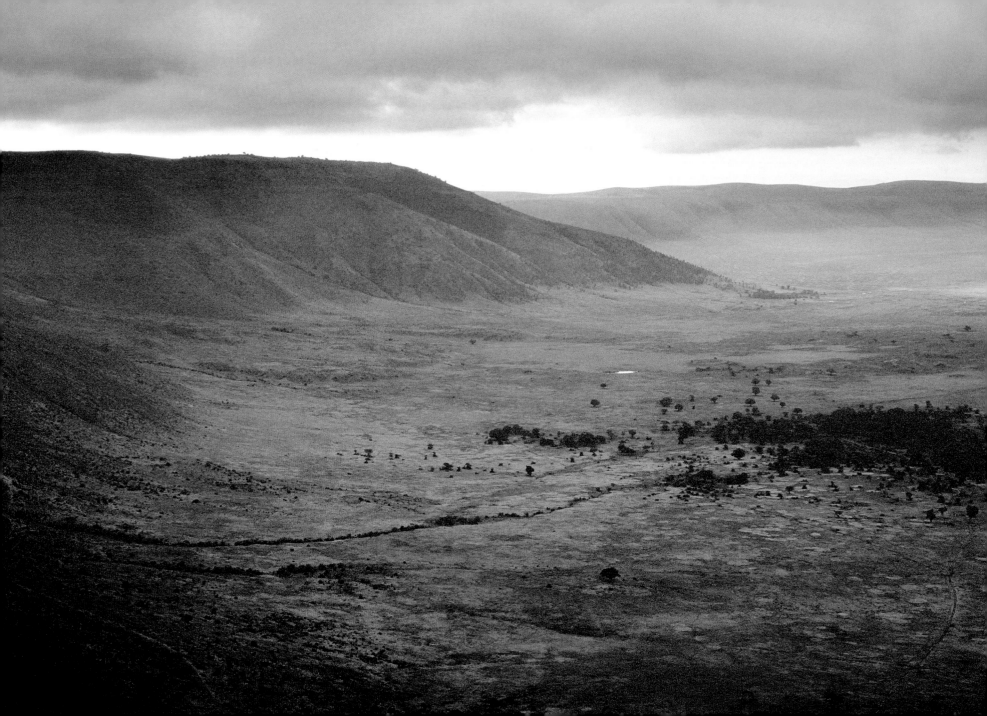

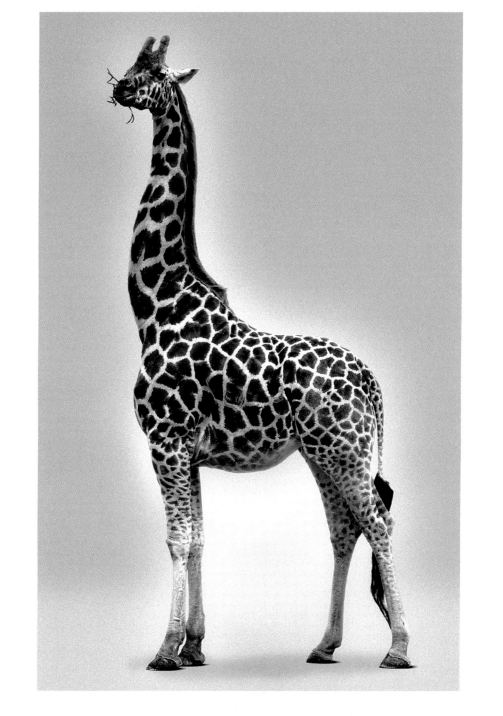

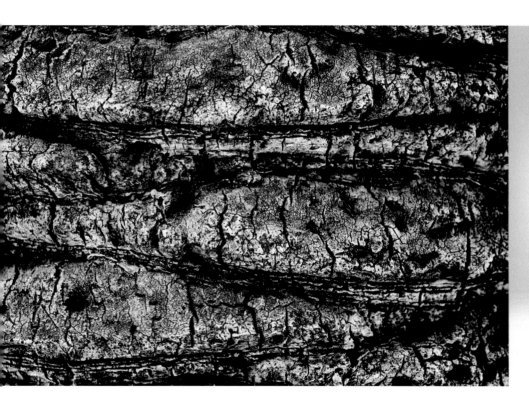
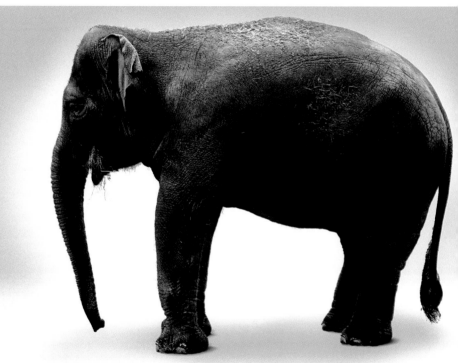

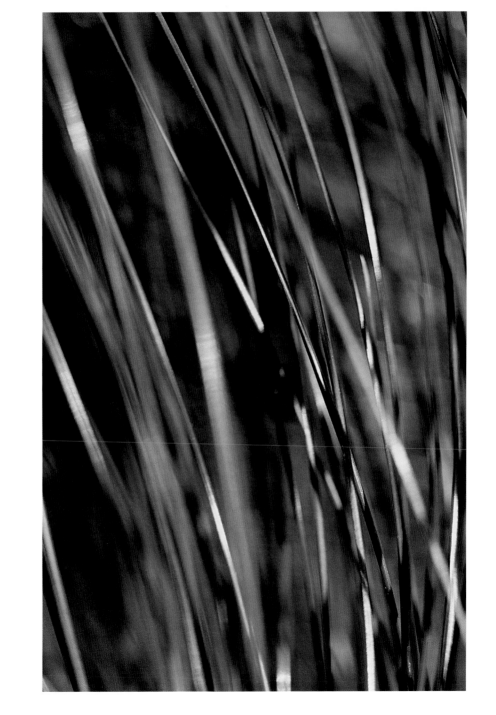

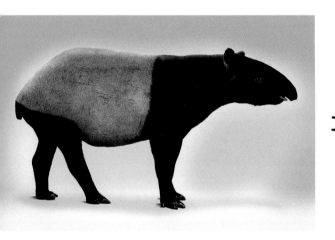

it seems clear that we have been doing t

you what we are on the verge of doing to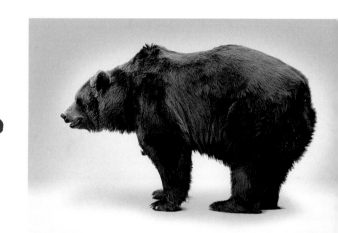

ourselves

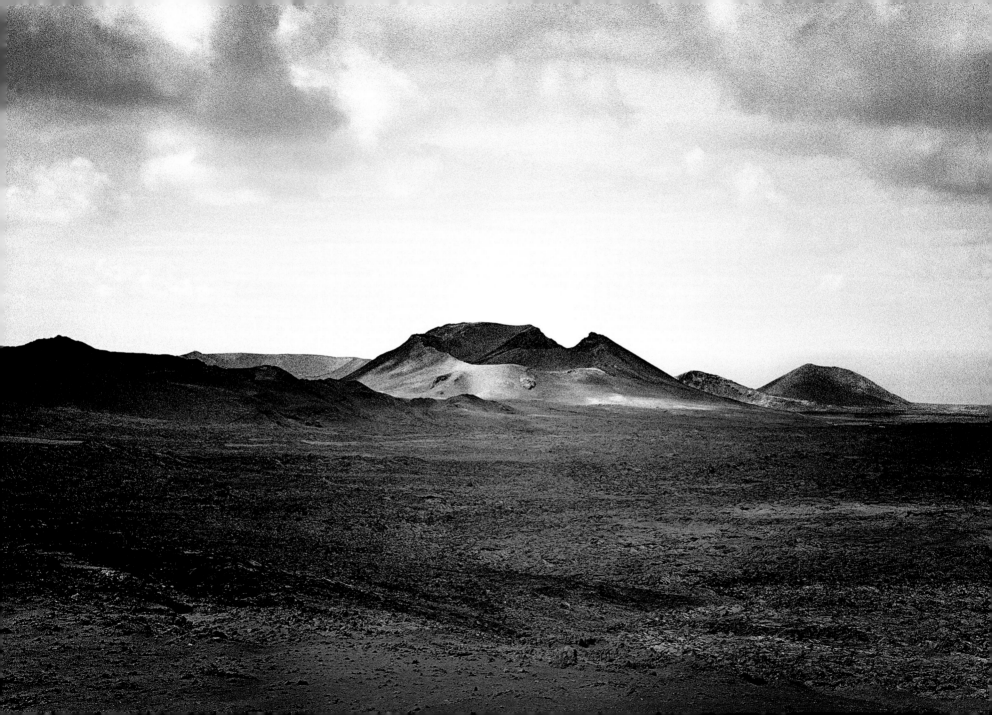

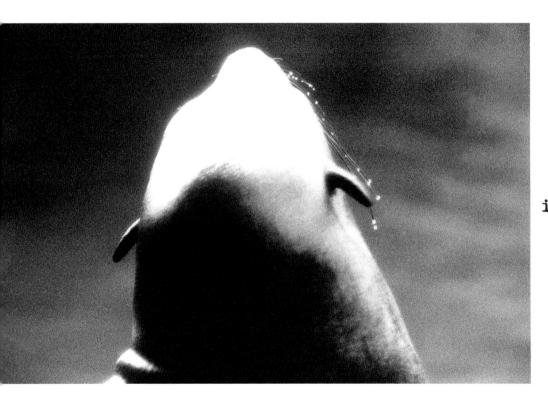

i hope you don't mind me telling you that you

strength

and craving for an

unrestricted existence

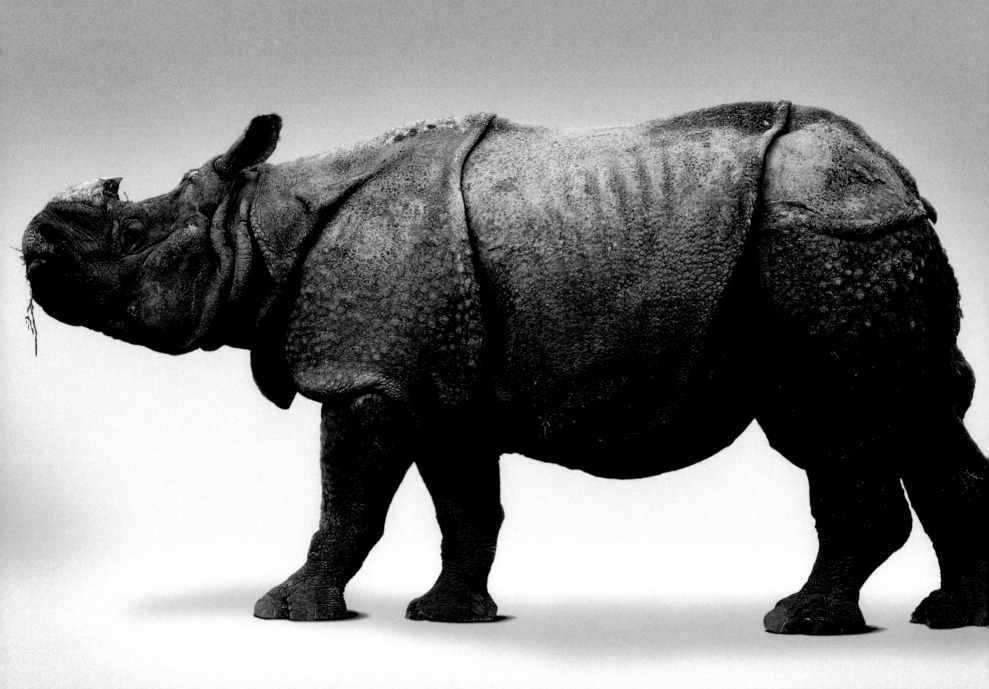

make you quite anachronistic

maybe that is why people consider you incompatible

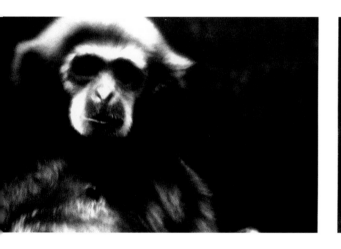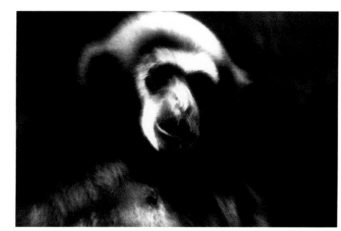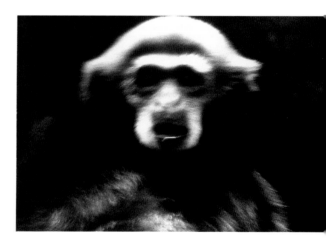

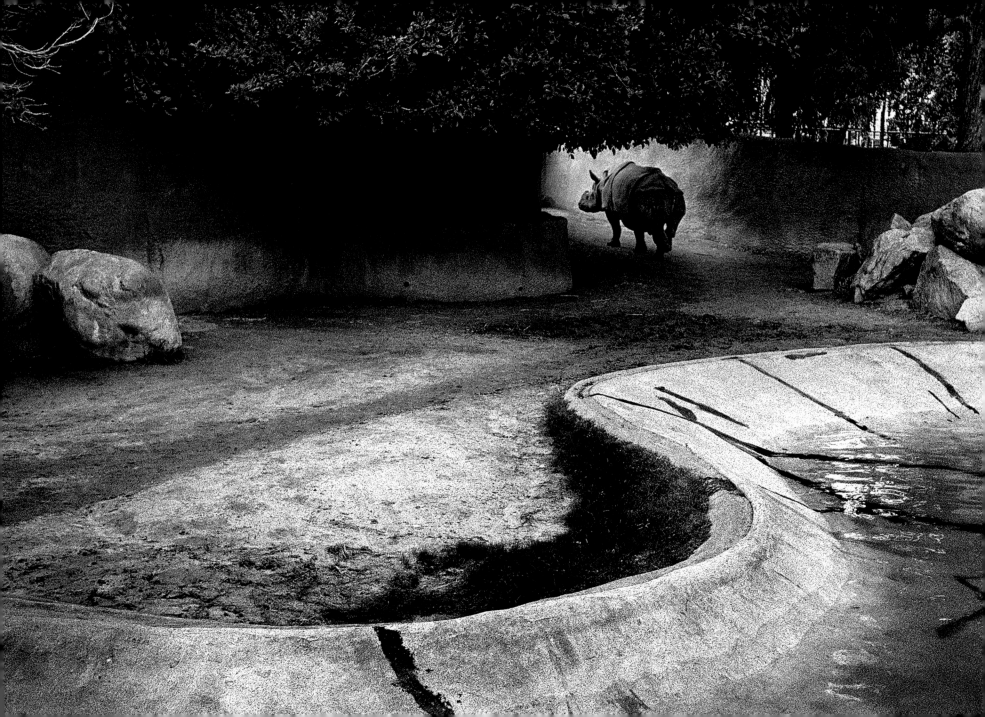

with modern times

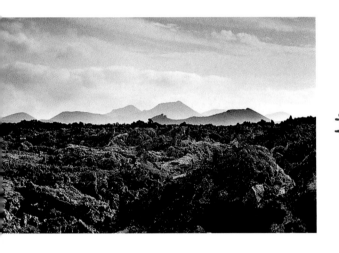

i have collected these images for all of u

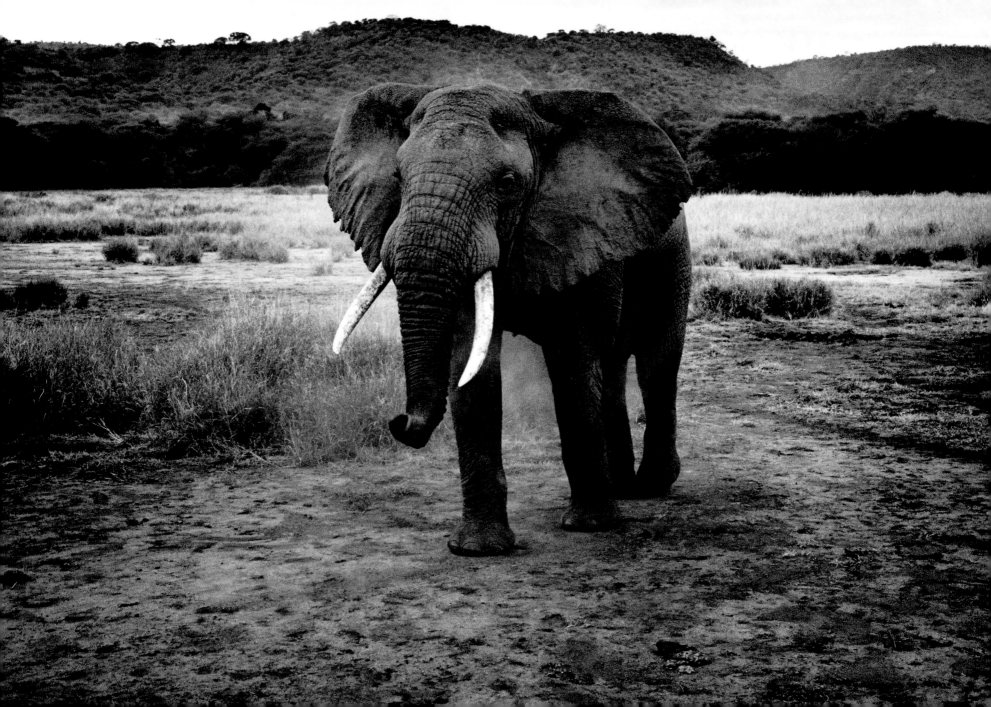

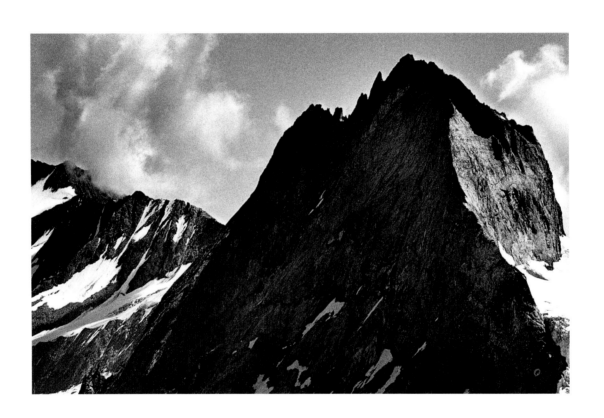

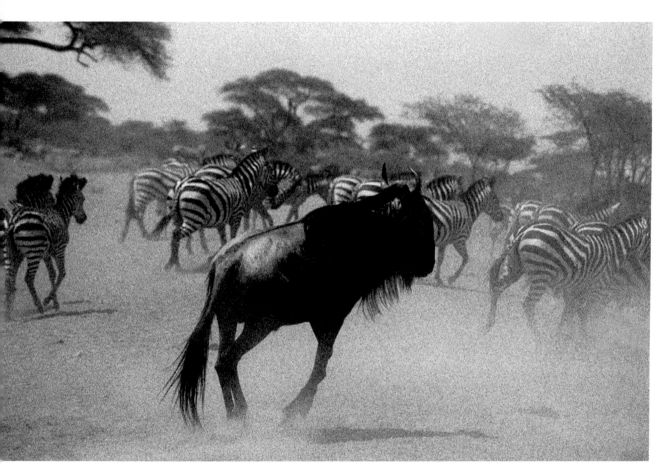

your devoted frien

this book is dedicated to ed and all things that remain wild

Acknowledgments

Thanks to the Jaschinski family, Reinhold, Waltraut, Peer, Karin and Lina; to my grandmother Inga Niessen (died 10 August 2002); to my friend and lover Edmund James and to all my friends for their emotional support.

Thanks also to Rainer Usselmann, Anna Fleischle, Boris von Poser and Steve Coleman for their expertise and technical support.

About the Author

Britta Jaschinski was born in Bremen, Germany and has lived and worked in London since 1993. Following the publication of her first book *Zoo* in 1996, her work has wo several awards and has been shown at many international art festivals and galleries.

ild Things

2003 powerHouse Cultural Entertainment, Inc. (American Edition)

riginal title: "Verehrte Tiere" published by Knesebeck Verlag 2003
2003 von dem Knesebeck GmbH & Co. Verlags KG, München
hotographs © 2003 Britta Jaschinski

ublished in the United States by powerHouse Books,
division of powerHouse Cultural Entertainment, Inc.
30 Varick Street, Suite 1302, New York, NY 10014-4606
lephone 212 604 9074, fax 212 366 5247
mail: wildthings@powerHouseBooks.com
eb site: www.powerHouseBooks.com

rst U.S. edition, 2003

brary of Congress Control Number: 2002116625

BN 1-57687-176-2

complete catalog of powerHouse Books and Limited Editions is available upon request;
ease call, write, or get wild on our web site.

0 9 8 7 6 5 4 3 2 1

rinted and bound in Germany